YOU CAN AFFORD TO DIE

Sensible Advice From a Practical Funeral Director

Revised

Joseph G. Kalmer

You CAN Afford to Die
Sensible Advice From a Practical Funeral Director
Joseph G. Kalmer
KMS Publishing

Published by KMS Publishing, Lebanon, IL
Copyright ©2019 Joseph G. Kalmer
All rights reserved.

No part of this publication may be reproduced, stored in a retrieval system, or transmitted in any form or by any means, electronic, mechanical, photocopying, recording, scanning, or otherwise, except as permitted under Section 107 or 108 of the 1976 United States Copyright Act, without the prior written permission of the Publisher. Requests to the Publisher for permission should be addressed to Permissions Department, KMS Publishing, joe@kalmermemorialservices.com

Limit of Liability/Disclaimer of Warranty: While the publisher and author have used their best efforts in preparing this book, they make no representations or warranties with respect to the accuracy or completeness of the contents of this book and specifically disclaim any implied warranties of merchantability or fitness for a particular purpose. No warranty may be created or extended by sales representatives or written sales materials. The advice and strategies contained herein may not be suitable for your situation. You should consult with a professional where appropriate. Neither the publisher nor author shall be liable for any loss of profit or any other commercial damages, including but not limited to special, incidental, consequential, or other damages.

Cover and Interior design: Davis Creative, www.DavisCreative.com

Publisher's Cataloging-In-Publication Data
(Prepared by The Donohue Group, Inc.)

Names: Kalmer, Joseph G., author.

Title: You can afford to die : sensible advice from a practical funeral director / Joseph G. Kalmer.

Description: Revised. | Lebanon, IL : KMS Publishing, 2019. | Previously published in 2010.

Identifiers: ISBN 9780983172611 | ISBN 9780983172628 (ebook)

Subjects: LCSH: Funeral rites and ceremonies--United States--Costs. | Funeral rites and ceremonies--United States--Planning. | Undertakers and undertaking--United States. | Finance, Personal. | BISAC: REFERENCE / Consumer Guides. | BUSINESS & ECONOMICS / Personal Finance / General. | SOCIAL SCIENCE / Death & Dying.

Classification: LCC GT3203 .K35 2019 (print) | LCC GT3203 (ebook) | DDC 393.0973--dc23

Revised 2019

ATTENTION CORPORATIONS, UNIVERSITIES, COLLEGES AND PROFESSIONAL ORGANIZATIONS: Quantity discounts are available on bulk purchases of this book for educational, gift purposes, or as premiums for increasing magazine subscriptions or renewals. Special books or book excerpts can also be created to fit specific needs. For information, please contact KMS Publishing, joe@kalmermemorialservices.com

This book is dedicated to the memories
of my two good friends/funeral
directors/business mentors,
Gary Bright and Dale Nichols.

You died two days apart eight years ago
and my heart is still heavy.
Your friendship, guidance, advice and
encouragement kept me moving forward.
I feel your presence every day
and for that I am grateful.

Table of Contents

FOREWORD VII

ACKNOWLEDGEMENTS. XVII

PREFACE: WHY I BECAME A FUNERAL DIRECTOR. 1

INTRODUCTION. 7

CHAPTER 1: VULNERABILITY 11

CHAPTER 2: FEDERAL INTERVENTION 15

CHAPTER 3: LET'S GO SHOPPING 19

CHAPTER 4: GOODS AND SERVICES. 23

CHAPTER 5: MERCHANDISE (CASKETS) 35

CHAPTER 6: MERCHANDISE (VAULTS) 43

CHAPTER 7: CLOTHING AND FLOWERS 49

CHAPTER 8: URNS 53

CHAPTER 9: CASH ADVANCES 57

CHAPTER 10: PRE-NEED 65

CHAPTER 11: CREMATION 71

CHAPTER 12: PLANNING AHEAD 79

APPENDIX 87

ABOUT THE AUTHOR 95

Foreword

Show me the manner in which a nation or community cares for its dead, and I will measure with mathematical exactness, the tender mercies of its people, their respect for the laws of the land, and their loyalties to high ideals.
–Sir William Gladstone

I've known Joe Kalmer his entire professional life. He enrolled in Mortuary School in 1987 and came to live in the funeral home where I was employed. In the Chicago area, some funeral homes house students while they are enrolled in mortuary school. They receive a room or an apartment in which to live and a salary, often meager, but an income, nonetheless. In exchange, the mortuary student assists the funeral home staff with any task that may be assigned to him, usually mundane or cumbersome ones that licensed funeral directors don't wish to do, and don't have to do, because they have a student. Mortuary students are at the very bottom of the funeral home hierarchy.

Joe was different from prior students. He was a quick study and he understood how the game was played: sort of a dues paying or rite of passage. After all, we all basically know how to do laundry, mop floors and wash cars! This new mortuary student we had stumbled upon not only handled the tasks given to him but wanted more. In a very short time after his arrival, Joe had mastered the basic tasks and was moving on to handling phone calls, assisting at visitations and funerals, and removing remains from their respective places of death. When a first call came in to the funeral home fifteen minutes before it was time to go home for the day, Joe was one of the first to grab his jacket and ask, "Where are we headed?" Joe was different. Joe cared about people, was of high moral character, and wanted to learn as much as he could about Funeral Service while he lived and worked with us.

Although I don't remember having the discussion with him, funeral directors inevitably ask each other in idle conversation the question, "Why?" Why does one choose this as a career? Is it because you have a calling to help people through some of the saddest and most difficult times of their lives? Is it because you enjoy the fact that no two days are ever the same—as they could be if you sat in the same cubicle in an office building day after day? Or is it because a substantial investment of capital, coupled with good old-fashioned hard work, might generate enough profit to provide a decent living for your family? I think Joe would have answered these questions like he answers all questions: honestly, with a hint of a twinkle in his eye, "YES!"

After his graduation, Joe went home to serve an apprenticeship in Edwardsville, Illinois. Upon completing that, he obtained his Funeral Director/Embalmer license and continued to work at that same funeral home—which he eventually ended up purchasing. After owning his own funeral home for several years which included a complete remodeling, Joe sold the funeral home to another firm in his town. He was employed by that firm, and was happy there, but eventually Joe came to the conclusion again that it was time for a change and moved on from there to begin his newest business venture, "Kalmer Memorial Services" in O'Fallon, Illinois.

Change is an essential element of success in anyone's career, or for that matter in the success of any business. Funeral Service is no different—there have been many changes since the ancient Egyptians began to mummify the dead. They believed that the body must be preserved so that the spirit might inhabit it again someday. During the next 1,500 years or so, advances were made in embalming—not specifically for burying the dead, but rather to preserve human tissue for anatomical research.

The Civil War brought great advances in Funeral Service. Embalming techniques were advanced enough to enable fallen combatants to be shipped home for burial. In all wars prior, the dead were for the most part buried on the battlefield in which they were killed. Following the Civil War, the assassination of Abraham Lincoln with his subsequent one month "funeral tour" of the country caught the attention of the general public. Embalming schools began to emerge to teach the art of embalming. Coffin companies were formed, often from the town furniture maker, to supply families with coffins to be used to bury loved ones. Some of these furniture store/coffin manufacturers went so far as not only supplying the merchandise for a funeral, but to "undertake" the task of handling the funeral proper. These "Undertakers," as they were now called, began to build buildings for people to gather for services after the death of a loved one instead of viewing the deceased in the "parlors" of their own homes. Funeral (Parlors) Homes were born.

Arguably, the latest change that has impacted Funeral Service is the internet. The internet was in its infancy when Joe and I were in school. However, it will now allow anyone with a modem instant access to information from across the globe. Information flows at lightning speed worldwide, true or untrue, for all to see and use. It is not uncommon for family members to bring various electronic devices along with them to the funeral home when they come to make arrangements.

While it is true that the many advances have occurred throughout history regarding the science of funerals, the reasons we hold funerals for our loved ones has pretty much remained constant. Funerals are for the LIVING. Funerals provide a means of closure for the immediate family of the deceased, as well as the community at large. They celebrate a life that was lived and allow friends and neighbors to show sympathy and support for the family at a sorrowful time. This holds true no matter what kind of funeral is arranged, as well as whatever your individual belief concerning what comes next for the deceased.

I would guess that cost is probably at the top of everyone's list of concerns when it comes to funerals. Maintaining the traditions that funerals have amassed over time can be expensive. Cemetery costs, casket, visitation, services, luncheon, flowers, etc. add up pretty fast. No one is denying the fact that funerals can be expensive, but a dignified funeral can be arranged much more economically than you might think. The key to this, in my opinion, is knowledge. The more you understand about a subject (in this case funerals) the better equipped you are to make sound decisions. Considering the circumstances in which you will be making these decisions immediately after the death of a loved one, knowledge is essential.

Knowledge can come from many sources. I think the best knowledge anyone can acquire comes from experience. You can read all the information you can find about electricity and current and grounding and may certainly understand the concepts, but nothing brings it home to be permanently implanted in your brain as the day you come in contact with an electric fence! The same holds true for funerals: you may read all you care to read, gather all the information you can, and still not have enough knowledge to make practical choices. On average, a person makes funeral arrangements less than six times in his or her lifetime. Hardly enough experience to be knowledgeable about the subject.

That's why a funeral director is such a great resource. He or she is a treasure trove of information regarding funeral services. They can not only arrange a meaningful funeral for your loved one, they can navigate the maze of local, county, state, and in some cases, international paperwork involved. Funeral directors, contrary to the beliefs of some, are not people who wring their hands when you enter the funeral home, ready to deplete the family resources. Granted, funeral directors are businessmen and women, but NO business shall remain in business for any length of time if they purposely force people into buying things they know they can't pay for. It's offensive and makes absolutely no sense from a business standpoint. We make a significant investment of time and money to build businesses, and more importantly, our reputations.

That's why I think this book needed to be written and needs to be read. My friend Joe is the perfect funeral director for this endeavor. Without sounding like a commercial advertisement, he is a knowledgeable funeral service professional with years of experience. Joe has gone from mortuary student to apprentice, employee, owner, and now owner of a new business and author. He has seen many changes in funeral service and is consistently on the cutting edge of new ways of serving the families that call upon him during times of great sorrow.

It is my sincere hope that you read this book and gain some insight on what being a funeral service professional means in today's world. Feel free to be entertained a bit by Joe's laid-back manner and ability to tell a story—he has a "down-home" air about him that will instantly put you at ease. More importantly, learn what it takes to run a successful business in an industry in which most of the clientele are facing the most difficult times of their lives. Take the knowledge gained from reading this book and think about your personal wishes and plans before the time arises. If you take nothing else from this book remember that there are professionals like Joe on duty 24 hours per day, 7 days per week, 365 days per year who are prepared for the honor of caring for your loved one and will, "with mathematical exactness" provide your family with practical, dignified, funeral service.

–John L. Rife, Crest Hill, Illinois

Acknowledgements

To Cheryl, Kelsie, Olivia, Cody and Lilly: Being the wife and children of a funeral director is never easy. Your love for me and respect for what I do are what keeps me going. You make it all worthwhile.

To my late parents, Sue and Norb: Thank you for life. Being raised in a home full of love, warmth, and kindness has made be a better man.

And to all my other friends and family, too numerous to mention, who have offered their advice, encouragement, sweat equity, support and prayers: Thank you, thank you, thank you.

To Dr. Michael Mulligan and Father Jeff Goeckner: Thank you for keeping me healthy: mind, body and soul.

PREFACE

Why I Became a Funeral Director

Thirty-one. If memory serves me correctly, that is the record. Thirty-one. As a young boy intimidated with the thought of leaving home the first day of kindergarten, my older sister had to think of a way to keep my mind occupied. She may have had the idea from our mother, but I don't know. Nevertheless, counting dead frogs on the streets of Germantown, Illinois from our home to our school six blocks away was worth a try. It worked. For whatever morbid reason, I was interested in those dead frogs. I guess in 1969, the climate was wetter, and the lakes were higher. Consequently, there were lots of frogs crossing the streets, apparently inattentive to the passing cars which were about to end their wet lives.

I had plenty to think about those first few days of the next phase of my young life: my first teacher, Mrs. Bohannon, new friends, the cute girl in the next row, homework, etc. But all I thought about were those frogs. Those *dead* frogs. I might have counted fourteen the first day, eighteen the second, and sixteen the third. After school, I would sometimes walk a different route and start the counting anew. Other times I would walk the same route and re-count. Were they still there? If not, where were they? Were they dragged off by dogs? Were there any more frog casualties? Why were some of them picked apart? I discovered the answer to the last question by witnessing a black crow nibbling away at one. That fascinated me. Although too young to know it, I was witnessing nature at its best. The frogs were born, they lived, they died. And if left exactly where they perished, they would rot and be eaten by other creatures in the food chain.

In due time, I noticed a lot of death: deer on the highway, cats on the street, dogs in the ditch, squirrels fallen from a tree. If it was dead and within sight, I noticed it. Not only did I notice it, I examined it. Not in a grotesque way; I would only poke at it with a stick and I would not, to the horror of my mother, bring it home. But I did look at it very closely. We didn't have an animal control department in our small town, so there were times when I observed the increasing level of decomposition; faster in the summer, slower in the winter.

Preface

Call it morbid fascination, I was attentive. I knew where they were. I would visit and revisit the site of their demise, anxiously anticipating whatever it was I was about to see. If left ignored, and satisfied that I had seen enough, I would take it upon myself to bury the carcass, giving it a "proper" burial.

In my teenage years I worked for the Youth Conservation Corps (YCC). The YCC was a group of young men and women who cleaned up our state parks, maintained campgrounds, rip-rapped ditches, built small walkway bridges, etc. Whenever we would find a dead animal, I was the one designated to "provide for its' disposition." I did so gladly. One day we discovered a raccoon in later stages of decomposition, maggots and all. My coworkers were amazed I could stare at the rotting animal while eating my lunch. That was the day I discovered the strength of my stomach; an attribute which would serve me well in the future.

Thinking back on my childhood and interest in all-things-dead, I could've gone another direction, off the beaten path. Another path may have led to a destructive lifestyle. Today my interest could be considered Gothic. The truth is, I was fascinated with the whole cycle of life. We, as do our canine and feline friends and other species, are born, live, then die. I believe science and religion will never agree on much, but I feel both are necessary. God creates life, then has doctors keep mom and baby healthy. What makes us live? What makes us die?

A while ago, while driving in the country, a rabbit darted out in front of me. I swerved to miss but didn't. One minute earlier that rabbit was alive and well, living his life to the fullest. The next minute that life was extinguished, snuffed out by a combination of his nerve and my driving speed. I didn't go back to "examine" the rabbit, as I would have as a boy. It did make me think about the days that were, the days that are, and the days that will be in a way I hadn't before.

For me, "the days that were", lead me to mortuary school. With my unique interest in death, I could've become a serial killer or a funeral director. Much to the relief of my parents, I chose the latter. It was a good fit. I wasn't taught about providing those animals with what's described as a proper burial, but it seemed like the natural thing to do. I felt someone must take it upon him or herself to dispose of the dead, whether it's man or beast, burial or cremation. People experiencing grief need honest guidance, professional and compassionate service. Your funeral director is the person for the job.

So, it all started with those first intimidating days of my elementary education. "Let's count the dead frogs, Joey." Indeed, I did, Beth. When I returned to Germantown, Illinois to visit my mother before she died, she talked to me about her own demise. It's part of a cycle. I still check to see if there are any frogs to count on my childhood streets, but I don't see them. They're still dead. They're just dead somewhere else. I guess the record of thirty-one dead frogs will forever stand.

Now that you know why I became a funeral director, I hope you learn from this book and find the answers to your questions about this whole dying business.

Introduction

Statistics tell us that in our lifetime we will probably make funeral arrangements four times. It may be for our mother, father, grandmother, aunt, uncle, close friend, or, God forbid, a child. I have already been on that side of the desk four times, and I'm not even sixty, so maybe those statistics are conservative.

As it is, my family gets off the hook easily when these times arise. As a funeral director, I know what we need, how to get it, whom to contact, how many death certificates we'll need, and the list goes on—that seemingly endless and bewildering list that involves Social Security, the VA, insurance companies, and any number of "incidentals" that need to be dealt with after someone dies.

I am always asked about the average cost of a funeral, which, in one sense is much like asking, "What's the average price of a car?" Just like cars, there are many types of funerals, but not every death will result in one. You have many choices: traditional funeral with a burial, cremation with a viewing, cremation without a viewing but with a service, direct cremation or "immediate" cremation with no service, anatomical donation, immediate burial and graveside service—just to name a few.

We can even add "green burial" to the list, the eco-friendly way to bury the dead: no embalming, a simple all wood casket or perhaps a gunny sack (literally, if allowed) buried in a shallow grave as quickly as possible. Many see it as a giving back to nature and take solace as flowers grow from the remains returning to the earth—"ashes to ashes, dust to dust."

When asked about the average cost of a funeral my reply is "about a fourth of the cost of an average wedding." That's right. And while some find it acceptable to spend $50,000 on a wedding that has 52% chance of failing, spending $12,500 on a funeral for the woman who gave them life is often considered out of the question.

What exactly is involved in the expenses for all the burial services? For example, if someone says they paid $12,000 for a funeral, the cost probably included cemetery expenses: grave space, grave opening and closing fees, temporary marker, and perpetual care—which could total $3,000 or more. This is often incorrectly referred to as "funeral expenses," not "cemetery expenses."

The consumer needs to know the difference, and that's part of my intent with this book. Just like the funeral itself, there are many choices at the cemetery. The funeral director controls none of them, other than informing the family and providing empathetic guidance in their decisions.

As a licensed funeral professional with over three decades of experience, I have acquired the skills necessary to embalm a body, put one back together after a traumatic death, and listen intently to those who are grieving. I have developed more compassion, become a more patient man with less of a temper, and have witnessed enough sadness that I thank God every day for simply rising from my bed.

I have learned to never take anything for granted because it could all end in an instant. Thankfully, I have learned this only in my role as a witness to life and death—not personal experience. I am truly grateful, and acknowledge my hope every day that it stays that way.

Because I have been richly blessed, I offer this book with the intent that it will enlighten you about the funeral industry. I'll share a few stories along the way—stories which I feel will accent my point and hopefully entertain you a little. Understandably, any time I share a story about a death or a funeral there is something morbidly comical about it. If it were not, it probably wouldn't be much of a story. But mainly I intend to inform you, the consumer, that you don't have to spend $12,000 on a funeral. There are ways to spend a lot less and feel like you've received just as much if not more.

It's not about being cheap. It's about being practical.

***Author's note:** There are many more women entering funeral service today than ever before, which is tremendous. However, in the interest in writing simplicity, I will refer to the funeral director as "he" in most cases.

CHAPTER 1

Vulnerability

Our media seem to think that every family who walks through the door of a funeral home is "vulnerable" because there has been a death in the family, that every death is tragic, and consumers can't think clearly when they are devastated. Well I have some news—not every death is tragic and most families I have guided through the years are thinking very clearly. In many cases, they are arranging the funeral of a relative who died in a nursing home, very old and afflicted with dementia; or perhaps a victim of a cancer which has ravaged their body. These are the family members who have been grieving for weeks, months, or years and are glad the battle is over. Though they may be uninformed consumers, they are not vulnerable. They just don't know the difference between a bronze casket, and one made of 20-gauge steel.

Batesville Casket Company makes a casket called the A 40 Primrose (about $3000). It's an 18-gauge steel casket with crepe interior. They also made the same casket in Solid

Bronze ($8000). My casket rep obviously wanted me to carry the Bronze. But with a wife, 2 kids and 2 mortgages, I could only afford the 18 gauge. A doctor came in and made funeral arrangements for his mother. "The Primrose" was located at the far corner of the room. From a distance, he pointed and said "I want that one. That's mom." I thought "darn, I could've sold the Bronze. He's a doctor. He can afford it." This man was a fine example of not knowing the difference in caskets, and at the same time, not caring either. But most people do care. And they should, because most families can't afford to purchase a casket without knowing the cost.

Of course, we realize that many families could be vulnerable and most of us in the funeral profession would never take advantage of it. Unfortunately, today we have many funeral homes that are part of large corporations. They have quotas to meet and reports to file with upper management. They have micro managers who don't seem to know when to back off. Large corporations have come in to small towns and bought out the "little guys." Now you don't see the owner of the local funeral home in church, at the grocery store or at

Chapter 1: Vulnerability

the summer-time festivals, because he is sitting behind a big desk in another state.

That's why, when it is one of those few times in your life you make funeral arrangements, it is important to know a little about the funeral home you have selected. Are they locally owned, and If not, who owns them? Who is your funeral director? How long has he been doing this? Does he show genuine compassion and is he patient, allowing you to make well thought out decisions? If you are not comfortable, ask for someone else. If there is no one else, go to another funeral home. Just because he did the embalming doesn't lock you in. The new funeral home will make arrangements for the transfer. His ego will only hurt a little and your comfort level is much more important.

One other thing to remember; it's not about the deceased or your friends. It's about you. If you want the funeral on Friday because you don't want to wait until Saturday, even though more of your friends can be there, do it Friday. Your friends need to re-arrange their schedules, not you. And speaking of Saturday funerals, the cemetery will be more expensive and so will the vault delivery fee. Make sure you know all the figures.

Don't be vulnerable. Be informed. There is so much more to learn, and I intend to teach you everything I can. Let's get started.

CHAPTER 2

Federal Intervention

The Federal Trade Commission (FTC) is very strict with our industry; to the point where it can be tacky to follow all their rules. Although we are required to hand out our "General Price List" when the family walks through the front door, I don't know of any of us who do. It's too impersonal. When we respond to a death at a residence, if the subject of cost is brought up by the family, we are required to hand them a price list at that moment. Not me. If they ask, I can give them approximate costs by adding in my head, and by doing so, I don't look like money is all I care about. I don't want my families to think, "Did you see that guy? He carries a price list for funerals in his coat pocket!"

I make it a point to show all my families the price list at a time I feel is most appropriate—before they select a casket, vault, urn or other merchandise. This way they have a figure about what they might spend that's fresh in their heads. Before we go into the "Selection Room," they know what they have spent so far because they know the cost of the services they have already selected. This is known as the "Service Charge."

Before 1984, funeral homes in this country didn't itemize their charges. They had one price for services with a casket. The FTC felt this was unfair to the consumer. It was too difficult to compare prices. Much to the chagrin of the funeral industry the FTC enacted what is known as "The Funeral Rule" that required itemized expenses.

Funeral directors had the typical reaction—too much government. We've been doing this for years. We don't want to change. It'll be too much work, etc. Of any profession I know, the funeral profession is slowest to change. The industry itself, however, is forcing us to change. Cremation is on the rise. There is much less attention to tradition. Funeral home loyalty went out the window as society's reluctance to spend came in to play. Funeral consumers are actually "shopping around." Oh my! Hence, the feds intervened and said we need to simplify our pricing.

Funeral directors ended up with a surprise. By itemizing they learned three things: 1) it didn't make the services any less costly; 2) they learned what it costs to provide those services, and it wasn't cheap; and 3) the consumer will shop for the best deal, even at the time of a death.

So, for the last 35 years, funeral homes have changed with the consumers by itemizing such things as basic services of funeral director and staff, transfer of remains to funeral home, automobiles, embalming, use of facilities, staff and equipment. The sum of these figures totals the "service charge." Basically, the service charge is the funeral home's operating expenses, or "overhead"—the word all business owners know. This is what it costs to run a business. In the funeral business, this annual figure is divided into the average number of calls the funeral home will do in a year.

Every business has fixed expenses—those recurring bills which are always there whether or not you have revenue generating business. Principal, interest, salaries, insurance, auto loans, phone bills, utilities, and maintenance are expenses which need to be paid on a monthly basis. If the sum of these bills is, for example, $50,000 per month ($600,000 annually), and the funeral home does an approximate volume of 125 calls per year, the service charge should be about $4800 per call.

So, for every adult-casketed funeral the funeral home performs, the family will be charged about $4800 to cover the overhead involved in providing that funeral. After all, the hearse, lead car and limo need to be clean, fueled, insured and driven, the building needs to be maintained with the yard mowed and the parking lot lit and free of litter, staff need be at the ready 24 hours a day, the embalmer needs to be paid well and the owner (and sometimes previous owner) gets his cut.

As long as there is a demand for these full-service funerals, funerals will not get any less expensive. Before the rise in the cremation rate and other less traditional forms of disposition, this was all the funeral industry knew. Yes, funerals are expensive because we are not in business to break even or lose money. But at the end of the day, our profit is no greater than the restaurant, service station, clothing store or barber shop down the street. Our hope is to show a 6% profit just like any other business.

CHAPTER 3

Let's Go Shopping

The term "funerals" covers a lot of territory. These days we hear it referred to as "Deathcare" because consumers are shopping for much more than just a funeral. Deathcare involves body donations to science, direct cremations, immediate burials, private services and other forms of disposition not having anything to do with an actual funeral or memorial service, which is an event with or without the body, when a life is celebrated. Therefore, when you, the consumer, are planning for the inevitable, there are some things you need to know.

When you call the funeral home on the telephone, the FTC requires the funeral home to quote prices if you ask. If they do not want to quote prices over the phone, they are violating the law and you should either report them, call another firm, or both.

If you go to the funeral home for a personal visit, they are required to show and explain their general price list, which you may keep if you so desire. If you are shopping for a casket, they must show you a "casket price list;" however, they are not required to allow you to keep it. Often, the casket price list will be laminated, indicating it is the property of the funeral home, which it is.

I'll let you in on a little secret. Remember that $4800 figure I explained in the last chapter? Well, since more of you are shopping around, that figure is sometimes deflated in the interest of competition. Does the funeral home lose money in providing those services for less? No. The difference is made up with the merchandise sale. If you want to know the bottom line, make sure you know what the casket costs and if it is the exact model quoted from the other funeral home. If you are truly shopping, (we usually have that figured out) ask us specifically and we'll tell you specifically, e.g., it's the R 59 Coretta. This way you can go to the next firm and get an accurate comparison.

For a business to stay in business, it must, at a minimum, cover its overhead. That's why a funeral home should recover its operating expenses and keep the cost of the merchandise lower. Why? Because in today's world, the internet is affecting our industry. Consumers can purchase a casket on-line and have it shipped to the funeral home; however, that online merchant can't pick up the body, transport, embalm, prepare obituaries or sign the death certificate. That's the job of the funeral director, and no, we don't like the online options, because our only profit is recovered from the sale of merchandise.

To remain competitive, funeral homes made yet another change: we developed "Package Pricing," the method of lumping all the service charges into one "package" and providing this package when the merchandise is purchased from the funeral home. This package will be considerably less than if itemized. It is not a "discount" and cannot be presented as such. This package must be specifically described on the General Price List. If all the service charges are added individually, instead of the $4800 figure described awhile back, it will add up to, for example, $5800. The minimum profit hoped for with a casket sale is, you guessed it, $1000. So, the family buys the casket from Costco and pays an additional $1000 for services. It's allowable because the FTC understands we need to make a profit.

CHAPTER 4

Goods and Services

The funeral contract is also known as "The Statement of Goods and Services." It is an actual contract which must be signed by the funeral provider and the person responsible for payment. It could be a legal-size document with 2 carbon copies, or it could be a contract generated by a computer. But nonetheless, they all have the same 3 categories: Services, Merchandise and Cash Advances.

Let's start with Services. As you know by now, the itemized services are supposed to cover the funeral home's operating expenses. But I need to explain each of these items separately.

"Basic Services of Funeral Director & Staff"

Consultation and arrangements with family, clergy, cemetery, florists and others as required; preparation of, filing and securing necessary notices, authorizations and permits; assistance with forms and 24-hour availability of staff. This fee will be added to the total cost of the funeral arrangements you select. This fee is already included in our charge for direct cremation, immediate burials and forwarding or receiving of remains.

This figure can be anything from $1800 to $3000. No matter what type of disposition is chosen, the funeral home will provide the above-mentioned service. Behind the desk and on paper, there's just as much work with a direct cremation as there is with a full traditional funeral. Because of this, this item is a **"non-declinable option."** It's important to remember that **every other item** associated with the funeral contract is a **declinable option.** It's also important to remember that this fee will be listed as included with the charges of direct cremation and "Forwarding and Receiving Remains," which will be explained a little later.

"Embalming"

Except in certain cases, embalming is not required by law. Embalming may be necessary, however, if you select certain funeral arrangements such as a funeral with viewing. If you do not want embalming, you usually have the right to choose an arrangement that does not require you to pay for it, such as direct cremation or immediate burial.

Chapter 4: Goods and Services

The above is taken directly from the GPL. The wording we use is very specific and highly scrutinized by the FTC, which has been known to do surprise visits to see if we are in compliance. Most funeral homes complain, but I feel it keeps us honest and only enhances our credibility with the public.

I wish I had a dollar for every time I've been asked the question, **"Is embalming a state law?" The answer is NO**. However, there are certain circumstances which would require embalming. Will there be a public viewing? If so, of course embalming is necessary and would have to be selected. An un-embalmed body is hazardous to anyone near it. In a matter of hours, the body starts to decompose and becomes offensive very quickly.

The Egyptians learned to preserve the body and eliminate the odors without interment or cremation. They became our first embalmers and eventually discovered "entombment." Today's embalmers accomplish the same results with preservation, but instead of a 40-day process, we can do it in about an hour and a half. Our method is not quite as thorough, but it is efficient. Embalming does not stop decomposition, it just retards (slows) it. Today's embalming methods retard decomposition long enough for the body to be viewed in a safe and sterile environment. Even though an embalmed body can be recognizable years after burial under the right conditions, it's not forever. I'll explain more of that when we talk about caskets and vaults.

Jessica Mitford, author of the 1960s best seller, "The American Way of Death," called embalming "barbaric." I strongly disagree. Embalming is simply as post-mortem procedure which preserves, cleanses, and sanitizes the deceased human body while retarding decomposition so the body may be viewed publicly. It is a very sterile procedure performed in an operating room-like setting by highly trained personnel who take their jobs as seriously as an artist would his subject.

"Does a body have to be embalmed if it will be cremated?" As the owner of a crematory, I get that question a lot. The answer of course, is no. But we have another "however." You might expect us to have a lot of paperwork. You're right, and there's considerably more with cremation. Why? Because once the cremation is performed, all the evidence is gone. The death certificate must be signed by either a physician or medical examiner/coroner, certifying the cause of

Chapter 4: Goods and Services

death. Then the "Coroner's Permit to Cremate" is issued, followed by the "Permit for Disposition," which is issued by either the city registrar or county health department.

Although today, we have "electronic filing," this paperwork can sometimes take several days to complete. Throw in a weekend or holiday and you'll add maybe another 2 days. Most funeral homes don't have refrigeration and therefore could require embalming: however, small town funeral homes usually will not require embalming in this case. They would place the body in a cremation container (usually made of cardboard), and wheel it in to the air-conditioned embalming room or another holding area, and "bend the rules" a bit. Large, corporate-owned funeral homes would probably view this as an opportunity to require embalming and charge for it. That's their right, but it's another subtle difference between the big guy and the little guy.

I could go on and on about other requirements for embalming, but I think you have the idea. The bottom line, embalming is *not* a state law and, in many cases, **may be declined.** But if it is selected, could cost anywhere from $500 - $900.

"Other Preparation of Body"

This is a fee on the General Price List and the Statement of Goods and Services related to the dressing, cosmetic application and casketing of the decedent. It goes along with embalming. However, even without embalming, this fee can be applied to the dressing and casketing of an un-embalmed body for Direct Burial, for example, which will usually be in the range of $250-$400. "Other Preparation of Body" also refers to doing these tasks after organ and tissue donation, which can complicate the embalming and dressing/cosmetic process. I advocate tissue and organ donations, but the process does add a lot of work for the embalmer, so this fee is quite understandable.

"Use of Facilities"

A visitation and/or funeral will be held in either the funeral home, church, cemetery chapel, or today, even in a banquet center. Obviously, there is a charge for this as well. You might wonder why the funeral home charges for a service at the church. After all, the funeral home doesn't own the church. He's not paying for the electricity to run the lights. True. But he is delivering the casketed body, setting up the flowers (sometimes dozens of pieces), and has staff on hand to tend to the register book, memorial contributions, parking, etc. This charge can be anywhere from $250 to $600 per day.

One way to cut back on the facilities charge is to do everything in one day.

Funerals are about celebrating a life. Visitations are about giving friends an opportunity to share a hug, shake a hand and remember the good times. All of this can be accomplished in three hours, unless of course the deceased is a well-known figure, which might prohibit my suggestion. But the average wake and funeral can be completed in one day. And it could save you $600.

My mother was a devout Catholic, but she was 91 when she recently passed away. Even with most of the friends of her five children paying their respects before the funeral, we were able to complete everything in one day, with the burial done by noon.

"Automotive Equipment"

Typically, a funeral home will provide 3 cars for a funeral service: the hearse (obviously), limousine, and lead car. The lead car is just that—it leads the procession and is properly marked. The lead car is also usually transporting the minister to the cemetery unless, of course, he's in the back of the hearse, in which case another minister would be aboard.

The charge for these automobiles could be $250-$350 each. One of the easiest things to decline is the limousine. In small towns especially, the cemetery is near the funeral home and paying for a limousine is senseless. If you're into that and want to be treated royally for a day, use it. But practically speaking, it isn't necessary.

A gentleman from Edwardsville named Ike died. Ike had been a gravedigger for over 50 years. Sometimes families choose a limousine for a selected group of people, such as pallbearers or grandchildren. Ike's grandchildren decided to, in lieu of the limo, all pile into Ike's backhoe for the trip to the cemetery. There were probably 7 or 8 kids in that machine, and they couldn't have had more fun. Hey, "We Put The 'Fun' In Funeral." And they saved $300.

This may surprise you, but the hearse is declinable. "Well what would we put the casket in, Joe?" The answer is the back of your pick-up truck, if you desire. Obviously, this doesn't happen often, but it has. I was working a funeral one day when the family decided to put the young man's casket in the back of his pick-up truck. We pulled the hearse out of line, put it in the garage and took it off the bill. And it couldn't have been more appropriate. You see, funeral directors are all about "personalizing" the funeral. Casket companies give us all sorts of ways to personalize, all at the added expense of the consumer. Well, what could be more personal than using one's own vehicle for his last ride?

Another vehicle may be defined as a "service utility vehicle." This is the funeral home van which is probably transporting flowers to the grave. Usually it is marked as "included," but trust me, it's built in to the service charge.

"Receiving Remains from Another Funeral Home"

When a funeral home gets a call from a funeral home in another state to pick up a casketed body at the airport, transport to the "receiving funeral home" and make arrangements for its burial at a local cemetery, this is called "Receiving Remains." This charge could be anywhere from $1200 - $2000. You might think that's a lot of money for such a small amount of work, but again, it's not cheap to own a hearse, insure it, put it on the road, pay a driver, assume the liability, etc. It's just the cost of doing business.

There's also the task at hand of coordinating the arrangements with the original funeral home, the airlines, the local cemetery, florist, minister, and vault company among others. And let's not forget the main job. Funeral directors must go to the cemetery, set the casket, and direct the service. This alone could take two hours from start to finish. In most states, you must be a licensed funeral director to provide this service.

It seems so easy; a trip to the airport and a trip to the cemetery. But there is so much more involved. These things may not be obvious to the consumer, but they are obvious to the funeral home owner.

"Forwarding Remains to Another Funeral Home"

If you have a winter home in Arizona, but primarily reside in the Midwest, for example, you should make arrangements ahead of time with your funeral home in the Midwest to "forward your remains" home. One of the biggest mistakes you can make when dealing with an out of town death, is to call *two* funeral homes instead of only one. Let the receiving funeral home, i.e. the one in the Midwest, be the one to make all the arrangements. This could save you up to $1500 or more.

If your intention is to have the funeral at "Midwest Funeral Home" but you personally call "Arizona Funeral Home," Arizona Funeral Home will view this as "a call," and you will be subjected to some of their service charges unnecessarily. Conversely, if you called Midwest Funeral Home and say, "Joe, my husband died. He's at Memorial Hospital in Anytown, AZ, and I need to get him home so we can have the funeral here. What do I do now?" The answer is, "You just did it. All you needed to do is call me." At this point, I will call a funeral home or an embalming service near the place of death and they will be subcontracted to do the removal and embalming. They will also arrange for the flight and transport the body to the airport. When we subcontract the work, it's done for a fraction of the price because only one funeral home is collecting the information for the obituaries and death certificates, and performing other administrative duties associated with the death.

Only call one funeral director—the one back home, the one you've known for years, the one whose kids went to

school with your kids, the one you've seen grocery shopping and at church. I hope I've made my point.

CHAPTER 5

Merchandise (Caskets)

The term "merchandise" includes a variety of items: caskets, vaults, register book packages, thank you cards, urns, flowers and jewelry. That's right, jewelry. We can take a thumbprint of the deceased, keep it in a file, and at any time in the future, you may come back and order a charm with mom's thumbprint on it, or a cigarette lighter with the same. Key fobs are another option, as are pendants with a portion of the ashes, which can be worn around the neck. "Oh, that's cute, what's in it?" "Oh, thank you. It's Mom." Some people think it's creepy. I say to each his own.

I remember meeting with a family who wanted a direct cremation with no service. "It was dad's wishes. He didn't want us to overspend." Then they proceeded to buy $2000 worth of jewelry. I have information on "thumbies" in my arrangement office. I don't even push it. It sells itself. Invariably, someone will pick up a brochure and say "I want this. How much does it cost?" I tell them the price and they usually order at least two. Is this crazy? Some would think. But it's not for me to judge. The industry is changing, and we need to change with it. If there's a demand, we will provide.

I'd like to think that every funeral director "teaches" while making funeral arrangements, explaining all your choices. But most people don't care what "cathodic protection" is, or if the bottom of the casket has a seamless weld. They care about how it looks. Is it pretty? Is it feminine? Is it masculine? Does the interior go with mom's dress? Well, on most selection room floors, all the expensive caskets answer those questions with a resounding "yes."

Casket company representatives advise funeral directors how to arrange their floors. What caskets to put where, highlight certain "price points," what kind of lighting, etc. And they should. That's their job. Most older funeral directors would rather have those reps stay out of their rooms, but in the newer days of marketing, merchandising, and price shopping, the younger funeral directors see the value in their advice. Funeral home owners would like to show a profit at the end of the year, and that profit comes directly from the merchandise they sell.

Chapter 5: Merchandise (Caskets)

Our casket room floors are merchandised no differently than a lot of retail stores. Lighting and placement of product are very important. That's why upon entering the selection room, the caskets that make us the most profit are highlighted. But you must remember, just because you don't see a casket doesn't mean it's not available. If they are too far from the distribution site, it may be in storage, and most funeral homes can receive it the next day. You need to ask.

Also, if you really like the solid bronze casket with the velvet interior but don't want to spend $8000, ask if they have a similar looking 18 gauge. It will be less than half the cost and no one will know the difference.

This brings me to another point. You, the consumer, need to know the difference in caskets, why they cost what they do, and what you can do to make sensible decisions when selecting one. There are basically 2 types of caskets, metal and wood. From most expensive to least, the metal caskets are made from the following materials: bronze, copper, stainless steel, 16 gauge, 18 gauge, and 20 gauge steel; the higher the gauge of steel, the thinner the metal. That's why 20-gauge caskets cost less than 16 gauge. Steel caskets rust over time, precious metal caskets do not. Does it matter? You be the judge. I personally think it doesn't, and I'll give you some reasons very soon.

From most expensive to least, wooden caskets are made from the following species: mahogany, walnut or cherry, oak, maple, pecan, pine and poplar. The wooden caskets you see on the selection room floor will be polished, well lit, made of the finest woods and have a plush, velvet interior. The corners of the casket will be inter-changeable so it can be personalized. You have many themes: golfer, fisherman, gardener, mom, dad, religious, military—you name it, we can personalize it.

Heck, we'll do 4 different corners if mom or dad had several interests. My most memorable experience came about 15 years ago. One family asked for 4 different corners: fisherman, hunter, dad, and a Christian cross. What made this memorable is where these corners were to be placed. They requested the fisherman and hunter be on the front where everyone could see. Dad and the Christian cross were on the back, because apparently, they were not as important to him. I thought about how his priorities were really messed up. I

Chapter 5: Merchandise (Caskets)

then told my wife if she ever has to select corners for my casket, put the dad and the Christian cross on the front.

Most funeral homes will display 15 - 20 caskets on their floor. But once again, you will not see everything that is available. You will see the casket they would like you to buy, but you might not see a price range with which you feel comfortable. There are very attractive 20-gauge steel caskets and there are very attractive poplar caskets. You just don't commonly see them, because they do not have the highest margins. Most funeral homes will remove a "cheaper" casket from its floor if it sells too much. I'll hear the funeral director say, "This one's too pretty" or "This one needs to be in a painted finish, so it looks cheaper."

But you have choices. Tell the funeral director the price range in which you are comfortable. And if you don't see the casket in the room, ask to see a catalog. He can probably show you books from 3 different companies and you'll soon have many more choices of those in your price range. And remember, your funeral director should always remain patient. If he isn't, ask to work with someone else. You should never feel pressured.

For me, the worst part of making funeral arrangements is taking the family to the Selection Room. I've never sold cars, but I would assume it could be fun. Selling boats is probably fun. Selling caskets is not fun. First, I'm a terrible salesman. I have a lot of respect for those who make a living on commission. I would fail miserably. You see, I can never "close the deal." No pressure from me. I truly feel I am an excellent funeral director because I'm a terrible salesman.

I just don't believe there's a need to spend $9000 on a casket when you can purchase one for thousands less which looks just as nice and will be buried in 3 days, never to be seen again. I can't tell you how many times through the years I heard a family say when selecting a casket for dad, years after mom died, "the only thing I remember was it was kind of a bronze color." They don't say, "Yes, Joe, do you still carry the Aegean Copper? Because we loved that one." And if the family doesn't remember, who the heck else will? Funerals are not the time to impress anyone, anyway.

One thing I hear a lot from families selecting a casket is the question, "Does it seal?" It seems that "the sealer" casket is of more quality than the "non-sealer," hence the need to spend

Chapter 5: Merchandise (Caskets)

more. I also hear this, "Well it's going to be in a vault, so we don't need a sealer casket." The truth is, you don't "need" anything. It comes down to what your beliefs are religiously, if you have any, and how you feel about how much the body is protected after burial. You can spend $10,000 on a solid bronze casket, put it in a $9000 concrete vault with a bronze liner and the body will still decompose. You see, there is this thing called anaerobic bacteria; the bacteria which grow without the presence of oxygen. Also, the body is 75% water and that water will escape to the bottom of the casket in a matter of months. Or you could spend $1500 on a 20-gauge non-sealer with a polished finish, put it in an $800 concrete box which the cemetery requires and let the aerobic bacteria take over. That's the bacteria which grow in the presence of oxygen. What about the $10,000 mahogany? Wooden caskets do not seal. Do you see what I just did? I took the expense from $19,000 down to $2300. As far as the physical decomposition of the decedent, it won't matter much (if it matters at all).

You see, if you're interested in protecting the body after death, you'll never get away from decomposition. That's not what God intended when He made us. Sealer or non-sealer, metal or wood, bronze or copper, we *will* return to the earth. It just might take a little longer in some cases.

CHAPTER 6

Merchandise (Vaults)

Buying a vault is less complicated than buying a casket, thankfully, but there still is much to know. Instead of 20 different choices, you'll "only" have about nine. It ought to be only three—good, better, best. Your nine choices will range in price from about $800 for that concrete box to about $11,000 for the concrete vault with the double bronze liner. In my career, I have never sold the latter and don't even offer it. I just don't believe in it.

In my funeral home/crematory, I've taken a much different approach to everything about this business. Unlike other funeral homes, I show only three: a concrete box, a concrete vault with a liner that provides "basic" protection, and a concrete vault which is heavier and made with a slightly better liner and a little more aesthetically pleasing, because you will see it for 15 minutes at the committal service, and that 15 minutes is just enough time for some people to impress their friends.

You'll notice I didn't call the first unit a "vault" because it isn't. It's a box; a box big enough to hold a casket. It also has a lid which fits on top but does not seal anything. **Although buying this box or a more sophisticated vault is not a state law**, the cemetery will usually require it for grave maintenance purposes. Simply put, graves sink, which makes it hard to cut grass. The grave doesn't sink as badly if the casket is encased. If you're interested in saving money and your beliefs permit it, ask the funeral director if an outer container is needed. Truthfully speaking, most families I've worked with do select one even if not required. This box will not keep out all the water, but it will keep out the dirt and protect the casket from the weight of the earth.

Wilbert Vault Company makes a vault called The Monticello. It's a fine vault made by a fine company which has been around for a long time. This vault will sometimes be described by the funeral director as a minimum vault providing "basic" protection. The word "basic" is used to imply although this vault is good, there are better vaults. But don't be fooled. This vault is made of concrete, has a seamless liner and has a lid with a tongue & groove seal. It's more than basic. It'll provide

Chapter 6: Merchandise (Vaults)

enough protection that Wilbert will give you a 75-year warranty, which is laughable to some. Who really cares? Will we dig it up when we're 108 years old?

The Monticello is usually displayed in a very bland gray color. The vaults which are more expensive will look much nicer on display. But the Monticello can be painted to match the casket. They will even highlight with gold or silver sparkles. The person's name will be on top and will have an appropriate emblem to go with it. This vault will usually retail for $1200 to $1500, depending on where you live.

If you want the casket to be somewhat protected and don't like the idea of ground water penetrating the seams of the concrete, this vault is an excellent choice. Don't let anyone tell you it isn't. Long before I became a funeral director, my uncle delivered and installed Wilbert burial vaults. He swore by that vault and when he died, my cousins chose The Monticello. That's what he would've wanted.

The next vault I will describe is called "The Venetian." It is two steps up from The Monticello. I skipped the one above it, called "The Continental" because it really is no different than The Monticello, other than it's heavier, a little nicer to look at and a couple hundred bucks more, because it's made with more concrete. If you're into looks and want to impress your friends for 15 minutes at the cemetery, which I don't agree with, The Venetian is the one for you. Of course, it's made of concrete, has a "marbelon" liner and has a carapace. It's a beautiful vault, but in my opinion, does not offer much more protection. This vault will cost between $1700 - $2100, again, depending on the area.

There are four or five more vaults above these, all heavier, fancier, double lined and *much* more expensive. Do I show them? No. And it would cost me nothing to do so. I would be provided the samples and they wouldn't take up much space. I just don't.

Vault companies have a fee to install the vault. Often the vault company sets the tent and chairs for the committal service. This fee can be a minimum of $250 and much more if it's a Saturday or holiday. When you see the price of the vault, this fee is not included because it's a service and not merchandise. Depending on the state in which you live, you're only taxed on the merchandise. Therefore, this fee is treated as a cash advance, which will be discussed in a subsequent chapter. When selecting the vault or concrete box, be sure to ask about this fee. You'll want to know how much more will be added to the bill.

Good, better, best. Arranging funerals can be complicated enough, especially when emotions are involved. Why complicate it even more by offering nine different vaults. Good, better, best. Concrete box, lined vault or lined vault that's a little fancier. All three serve different purposes and do the job that needs to be done.

CHAPTER 7

Clothing and Flowers

"We'd like the flowers to match Mom's dress." This is a sentence I've heard countless times, so, I thought I'd talk about clothing and flowers in the same chapter.

"Burial garments" provided by a funeral home, are exactly as you would imagine—morbid. For women, different shades of pink, blue, and green with lace collars, a high neckline, long sleeves and, by necessity, slit down the back. (It is virtually impossible to dress a stiff, deceased human body without the assistance of scissors.) A man's suit is less morbid, because it's just a suit; an overpriced suit, but a suit, nonetheless.

The dresses are also overpriced and, did I say they were morbid? When asked about clothing, I *always* suggest my families bring in their own clothing if possible. You might wonder, if some actually do *not* have any clothing. The answer is yes; most notably older folks who die in a nursing home. Many times, they have nothing but hospital gowns and sweat pants. If they need a dress or a suit, or jeans and a tee shirt, I suggest going to the local department store to get something. If I'm going to sell them something, I must make $100 on it. And to be fair, they'd do much better going to Wal Mart. Remember how I said the vault will only be seen for about 15 minutes and then forgotten. Well, the clothing will be seen for several hours, but again, who are you trying to impress? Let's be practical.

"Do I need to bring in underwear, shoes and socks?" Yes. It's a human body and we funeral directors treat it with respect. I say "it" because everything that made that person Mom or Dad is gone, but it's still Mom or Dad. I should know. I embalmed my own father, and my father-in-law. And like the thousands of other bodies I've embalmed and dressed in my career, they had on underwear, shoes and socks.

Bring in the deceased person's clothing. If not, go out and buy some from somewhere else. Don't overspend. Remember, it'll only be seen for a short while.

Flowers are an interesting subject, especially for the funeral director. His relationship with local florists should be one of peace and serenity. After all, he sends a lot of business to the florist. But this relationship is sometimes strained.

Chapter 7: Clothing and Flowers

Usually there are many more floral shops than funeral homes in the same town. They all compete for funeral business, because like weddings, people spend money for flowers on funerals.

I've seen many funeral directors grumble about selling a cheap casket, and then the florist shows up with $1000 worth of flowers. I try to remember it's all about priorities. I'm just happy to get the funeral because, like florists, we have competition ourselves. As one of my retired funeral director friends once said to me, "All funerals are good funerals." I don't care if it's a 20-gauge non-sealer or a solid bronze, I couldn't agree more.

Funeral directors will usually give you a choice: you can order the flowers (casket spray and other family pieces) or they can order the flowers and then put them on the bill. "Put them on the bill" is usually selected. We'll pay the florist for you. Isn't that nice? The florist gets their money and we could get stiffed (no pun intended). It's all about service and if there is ever a service-oriented business, it's the funeral business. (Do you see sometimes how the relationship can be strained?)

I personally have never owned a rented casket spray. It's too impersonal. I like being practical, not cheap. There's a big difference. Get some fresh flowers. You don't have to overspend, but a couple of hundred bucks will add beauty to a sad situation. If $200 is too much, you can get a nice arrangement, only smaller and in a vase, for $75. It's a nice touch and it's not that much.

CHAPTER 8

Urns

Urns hold ashes. "Ashes" is a somewhat misleading term. When I think of ashes, I think of the remnants of a cigarette which literally blow away if subjected to the wind. In our world, ashes are the cremated remains of a deceased human being and are more the consistency of sand; very granular and a bit heavier.

When a cremation is finished and the retort (oven) is cool enough to be opened, all that is left is a pile of bones—the only non-combustible part of the human anatomy. Depending on how the body was clothed, also included will be metal snaps, hooks or zippers, and certainly artificial knees, hips and other surgically implanted devices. If the decedent had a pacemaker or defibrillator, it would have been removed by the embalmer. These devices would explode during the cremation and could damage the equipment. The bones and other items are then raked into an "ash-pan" and poured onto the lid of a "processor." These items are separated from the bones via a powerful magnet and disposed of unless told otherwise.

Once the operator is confident the only thing left on the lid are skeletal human remains, the remains are swept into the processor. The lid is placed on the processor and the power is switched on. The processor runs for thirty to forty-five seconds and presto, we have "ashes," or at least what's called ashes. Obviously, these ashes must be placed in some sort of a container.

If an urn is not selected, the ashes are placed in a "temporary container" which is a black or a brown heavy plastic urn with a clear plastic liner (like a freezer bag). The word "temporary" implies that it isn't suitable for anything except to hold the ashes until a more expensive urn is chosen. Before another urn is chosen, it's good to consider what you'll be doing with it. Will it be placed on a mantel? If so, purchasing a more attractive urn would be appropriate. Will it be buried? If so, an "urn vault" might be required by the cemetery for the same reasons a casket vault might be required. If this is the case, there would be no reason to purchase anything other than the vault. Most would think it's silly to buy an expensive

Chapter 8: Urns

urn, only to be placed in a vault at the funeral home or crematory, never to be seen again. If a vault is not required, this "temporary urn" could be directly buried. It's durable enough to withstand the weight of 18 -24 inches of dirt.

Wilbert Vault Company makes an urn called "The Tribute." It's made of a marbelon material. It looks pretty enough to be displayed on a shelf and is durable enough to be buried without a vault. Most cemeteries would accept this urn without the need to purchase an urn vault. So, if you want something more than the plastic box urn but don't want to spend a lot, this is an excellent choice. I sell this urn for $210.

I recently handled the cremation and memorial service of a 53-year-old man named Jack. His 81-year-old father chose to make his urn. It was a "double-wide" with a space for Jack's wife, who will be cremated after her death. This is perfectly acceptable. He made a beautiful urn, tasetefully handcrafted and made with love and compassion.

Just like caskets, you'll see a variety of urns. Just like the caskets, you'll see the urns displayed that they hope you'll buy. But again, there are many more choices in the catalogs the funeral homes carry. If the funeral home doesn't carry the style of urn you like or isn't in your price range, peruse these catalogs.

When one thinks of an urn, the picture that comes to mind is a vase. It will have a "curvy" figure with a fancy lid. The truth is, this is only one kind of urn. Everything from a wooden chest to a brass cube, a clock to a bronze dolphin, or a porcelain urn with a religious theme to a bio-degradable urn made from earthen clay. "So many choices, so little time." Oh, how untrue! Cremation affords you the time to make decisions. Decide what you want *after* you know what you need.

CHAPTER 9

Cash Advances

I've been to so many seminars through the years sponsored by consultants who make their living telling us, as funeral home owners, what we're doing wrong. We are so focused on "service" that we forget at what cost. "You've created this monster," they'll say. And they're correct. "If my competitor pays for the funeral luncheon and has to wait thirty to sixty days to get paid, well, by God, I will too!" At least the restaurant got their money today. "If my competitor pays the $1000 grave-opening fee and has to wait thirty to sixty days to get paid, by God, I will too!" At least the cemetery got their money today. Meanwhile, the families we serve think we're the greatest thing since sliced bread.

Most families do pay within thirty to sixty days. Some families pay sooner. And, hallelujah, some pay immediately! But guess what—some don't pay at all. But at least the restaurant and the cemetery, the minister, musician, the hairdresser, and the newspapers got paid today—by the funeral home.

The vault or concrete box installation fee previously discussed should be treated as a cash advance, so you won't have to pay sales tax. If this fee is included in the price of the vault, ask the funeral director to separate this charge so the tax is less, unless of course your state taxes for "services rendered."

The obituary published in the newspaper is a cash advance with a cost you can sometimes control. I say "sometimes" because the longer the obit, the higher the cost, obviously. This is particularly true with newspapers in large, metropolitan areas. Smaller towns, however, sometimes have a set fee—often as little as $25 no matter the length—while other small towns don't charge at all.

When going over the obituary information with your funeral director, ask which papers charge and how much, because the fees will vary. An obituary can easily be edited to a reasonable length. For example, if it is submitted to the *Chicago Tribune* because the person lived there 40 years ago, there would be no need to list the names of all the survivors or the person's work history. His old friends in Chicago don't need to know that he was a member of the local Senior Citizens Center or a 4th Degree Knight of Columbus. What they need to know is to whom he was born and what other connections he had to the city.

Today, almost all funeral homes have a website. And the main purpose for this website is to post obituaries. It's also important to remember how social media such as Facebook contributes to "spreading the word" about a death. Newspapers are feeling the squeeze, because so many will eliminate the paper obit in lieu of social media. And social media is *free*.

All cemeteries have a "grave opening and closing" fee. This, of course, is the cost to dig the grave and fill it back in after the burial. This is another charge that varies. A small rural cemetery might still dig the grave by hand (seriously) and only charge $225, while the large privately-owned cemetery uses a backhoe and charges $1600. You might think, "$1600? It only took him 20 minutes." True, but the cost to run the backhoe, insure it, pay the operator, etc., is not a small expense. Cemeteries and gravediggers have overhead just like funeral homes. Remember my story about Ike, the gravedigger? He was an absolute magician with that backhoe, but it came at a price. After all, I couldn't jump in there and do it. I had a burial at a local cemetery which was known for its hills, and this particular winter morning the grave was located near the bottom. There was no way I was going to get my hearse near the grave with all the snow and ice. Ike said, "Put it in my bucket. I'll get it down there." I was a bit reluctant, but I trusted his judgment. Ike got that hardwood casket down to the grave without a scratch. At the time, the grave opening fee was $600. I'd say it was worth every penny.

Some years ago, I had a burial near Ottumwa, Iowa, the fictional home of Corporal Radar O'Reilly from the M*A*S*H television series. Since it was about a 6-hour drive, I drove there the day before. A good funeral director always makes a dry run to an unfamiliar cemetery. When we are leading a funeral procession, our biggest fear is making a wrong turn. I know of one funeral director who didn't make that dry run, and not only did he make the wrong turn, he led the procession to a dead end (no pun intended). Thirty cars had to stop, turn around and start over. That's almost as embarrassing as getting to the cemetery and realizing you forgot to order the vault.

At any rate, this burial in Ottumwa didn't require a procession, but I did need to know where it was to ensure that I would arrive prior to the family on the day of the burial.

Chapter 9: Cash Advances

Upon my arrival at the cemetery the day before, I noticed a gentleman sitting in his truck eating an apple. Meanwhile, an elderly woman was in the grave with a shovel. The gravedigger's name was Mr. Williams. I asked the gentleman in the truck, "Should I have written this check to Mrs. Williams?" He said, "She's a fine woman." I wonder if Mrs. Williams thought $400 was enough.

People ask me all the time what a minister should be paid to conduct a funeral. It will vary from nothing to a few hundred dollars. It just depends on the minister and the situation. I usually give the minister a minimum of one hundred dollars. Some would argue that Mom or Dad gave to the church every Sunday for the last 50 years so the minister should do it for nothing. Maybe, but this minister might only have been there for the last two years or so. Also, he or she is rearranging his or her schedule to accommodate the family and is probably putting in a great deal of time to prepare so the funeral is personalized. Most clergy like to meet with the family for a few hours a day or two before the funeral, especially if they don't know them well.

Although this is true in most cases, I've worked with clergy who didn't deserve anything. I remember one minister in particular. He would arrive at the service at 9:45, ask for an obituary, read it, ask me how to pronounce certain names, walk in at 10:00 and have the most generic funeral you'd ever witness. I always said that's the easiest 100 bucks anyone could make.

Musicians are another cash advance which will depend on the situation. Typically, musicians shouldn't be paid as much as the clergy, but they do deserve a generous stipend. Again, you might think, "A hundred dollars and all they did was play one song?" Yes, but let's think about this. I'll use my dad's funeral as an example. My mom wanted "Oh Danny Boy" played on the trumpet at his funeral. I contacted the music department of Southern Illinois University at Edwardsville. A man by the name of Mr. Anderson drove the 40 miles to the church and belted out a beautiful version of Oh Danny Boy after communion. It was a tremendous gift to my mom and a wonderful tribute to my dad (who was quite a talented musician). He was paid $200, but it was probably worth more.

Chapter 9: Cash Advances

Cash advances are a convenience for the family. Because of our generosity, families don't have to write seven or eight checks and disperse them as needed the day of the funeral. Whatever the amount due the minister, musicians, hairdresser, etc., is the amount on the contract. If there is a charge for handling these fees, it must be noted. But typically, there isn't.

I was taken aback once by a family who told me of the conversation they had with a sexton at a local cemetery. In addition to the grave opening and closing fees, this family had to purchase the grave space for a funeral to be held in the next few days. When asked about paying the cemetery, the sexton informed them, "If you don't want to pay now the funeral home can take care of it, and you can settle up with them." Needless to say, I had a talk with the sexton.

If I can't get paid within thirty days, I require my families to at least pay for the cash advances. It's only fair. That's money out of my checkbook. When I have a family suggest paying this fee before I share my policy, I know I'm dealing with a family that probably owns a business. They understand. It's still a convenience. After all, they only have to write one check today instead of seven or eight.

CHAPTER 10

Pre-Need

Back in the seventies, arranging for your funeral ahead of the need came into vogue. It really wasn't started by the funeral homes, but rather by the folks who wanted to make sure their wishes were carried out and the "burden" lifted from their families. To this day, these are the two main reasons "pre-arrangements" are still being done.

At some point, probably in the late seventies and early eighties, consumers started to pre-pay their funerals with the guarantee the price will be "locked in." We started to see the potential market for this, so insurance companies jumped in and said, "We'll fund it for you." Banks also said to the funeral home, "Bring your pre-need money to us and we'll set up a trust. You decide if it will be a 16-month or a 12- month certificate of deposit. Just take the higher interest rate."

State laws were enacted so we became the "trustees," which allowed us to keep part of the principal and interest. In Illinois, for example, when depositing the money from the consumer, we can retain 5% of the original principal and 25% of the annual interest. These fees were due us because we maintain these accounts, make deposits for the consumer as needed, report to the Comptroller's Office annually, etc.

If you think this is excessive, let me tell you a story. Many years ago, a little lady from Edwardsville came to my office and wanted to pre-pay her cremation. At the time, the total bill would have been around $1200. She started with an initial deposit of $100 and wanted to pay $25 per month until her contract was fulfilled.

Every month on or around the third, I would get a $25 check in the mail from Evelyn, followed by a phone call from her asking, "Joe, did you get my check?"

"Yes Evelyn, I did."

"Did you deposit it yet?" she'd ask.

"Not yet, Evelyn, but I'll get it there today."

After about two and a half years of these monthly trips to the local bank, and a grand total of about $950 with interest, I told her in her monthly call to me, "Evelyn, guess what? It's all paid. You don't owe any more."

"Really? I thought I had a little more to go."

Chapter 10: Pre-Need

"Nope. It's taken care of."

When she died, I was a little short, but she got just exactly as she wished, and I thought of those 12 trips I *didn't* have to make to the bank.

Another little lady named Loretta never married. She was known to be worth several hundred thousand dollars, if not more. I can't count the times she came to me and said, "Joe, I need to talk to you about my arrangements." Being a young owner and eager to do business with anyone, with or without money, I would anxiously reply, "Anytime Loretta. Please give me a call."

After no less than a dozen of these exchanges over a three-year period, (I told you I wasn't very good at this) I finally said, "Loretta, how about next Tuesday?" (Apparently, I'd been to a recent sales seminar.) She said, "No. I don't think that will work. My nephew will be in town." After several other casual attempts, I finally decided Loretta did not want to let go of her money, not even for her own funeral; which is precisely why she had the money she did.

Loretta died a few years later. I handled her funeral and was paid quickly by her estate. I placed her in a **simple**

20-gauge steel casket and the Monticello vault. If you remember, the Monticello is **simple**, but very good. It was a very **simple** funeral; just a few friends and family with everything completed in about 3 hours. The burial was in a **simple** country cemetery on a beautiful summer morning. The only thing not simple was her willingness to pre-pay while alive. So, you see, the fees we collect can also make up for the fees we'll never collect despite our efforts.

In addition to pre-paying and pre-arranging to ensure your wishes are carried out, and along with eliminating the "burden" from your family, it could be important to plan ahead if there is a "spend-down" situation. If a person is in a nursing home and their care is being paid with the individual's own money, it's quite likely that money will be exhausted before the person dies. Nursing care is not cheap. $3000 per month is on the low side. If one is not independently wealthy, he or she will outlive the money. Many states will allow that person to "spend-down" by pre-paying their funeral. All their assets must be exhausted before state aid eligibility. No house, cars, life insurance cash value or other assets are allowed. A person may have a limited amount of cash necessary for "daily living." In Illinois it's not to exceed $2000. This fund can be used for things such as clothing and a weekly hairdresser. If the pre-paid service with the funeral home is "irrevocable," it is allowable to spend this money before the need arises, and smart to do so.

CHAPTER 11

Cremation

Funeral home owners grumble because they have a garage full of expensive cars, a staff with little to do, and property taxes on a 7000 square foot building, all while working within a 50% cremation rate. The grumbling can be just as loud from casket manufacturers for obvious reasons. That's why casket companies decided to start selling urns. They also started teaching funeral homes how to make money selling cremations.

Casket and urn manufacturers encourage us not to assume cremation to be cheap with no type of funeral service. So now, even though cremation might be the ultimate form of disposition 50% of the time, families are given the choice of viewing prior to cremation, either private or public, because viewing provides "closure." It's part of the grieving process and necessary for healing.

When arranging a cremation, you'll have more choices than you would have imagined. By law, the body must be placed in some sort of cremation container. This doesn't mean a casket. It can be as simple as a cardboard container. The reasons for this are that crematory operators don't have to be licensed funeral directors or embalmers, and they may not be trained to handle deceased human bodies. Also, unless the body is in a container, there would be no dignified way for the body to enter the chamber.

In the old days, funeral directors wouldn't give you a choice. They simply assumed you'd want the minimum container. And if they charged enough, which most had done, they didn't care. But today, this will be explained to you. Which container or casket will you select? I don't advocate just the cardboard box. I also don't discourage it. If you are to have a private or public viewing, you may want to select something a little more dignified. You'll find a cremation casket that looks nice for well under $1000. And if you think it looks so much cheaper than an expensive casket, well, it is. But remember what you're there to do. This is not a traditional funeral so why go to that expense? You're being totally respectful even though you're selecting something much less expensive.

For those who feel viewing is not necessary, I hope you're right. You probably are, but there's no turning back—cremation is irreversible. If it is right for you, the minimum cardboard container is adequate. It will retail for under $100 and is usually sturdy enough to get the job done with dignity. If a person is 250 pounds or more, something sturdier may be necessary. The crematory operator doesn't want any accidents. Many cremation caskets, starting in the neighborhood of $800 are strong enough to hold 500 pounds.

Cremation Providers

In today's market, we have different types of cremation providers:

Traditional Funeral Homes – These are the funeral homes which are long-standing members of the community, whose main business through the years has been traditional burial. Only in the last 20 years have they been adjusting to the rise in cremation. Usually, their prices for "Simple" or "Direct" cremation will be quite a bit more expensive. They have more business overhead (operating) expenses than less traditional providers. It's not uncommon for their charges to be $3000 - $5000 for the basic cremation services.

Professional Discount Providers – These are the businesses which focus on cremation arrangements. Their fees are much less because they usually operate out of a smaller office, often rented space in a strip center. They usually outsource the cremation, so they don't even have the expense of operating the machine. The advantages to these providers are they are much less expensive because of their lack of overhead, and you still receive the personal touch from licensed, local funeral directors. Their fees will usually be in the $800 - $1600 range.

Internet Providers – Since almost all of us have access to the world wide web, there are now providers who operate with nothing more than a website. You go on-line, fill out the information, pay with a credit card and you are finished. Sometimes you don't even speak to a funeral director, much less meet him. He may be a thousand miles away. This provider will outsource everything from the transportation of the deceased to the actual cremation. The death certificate must be outsourced, as well, since it must be filed where the death occurs. If the consumer has questions or concerns, or if mistakes are made, it can be difficult to get a return phone call or resolve an issue. They might only charge $595, but you get what you pay for. Be careful.

Cremation Options

Full Service Cremation

With a full-service cremation, think of a traditional funeral/burial, but everything ends before you go to the cemetery. When you make arrangements with the funeral director, you will likely select services such as Professional Services of Funeral Director and Staff (non-declinable), Embalming, Other Preparation of Body, Use of Facilities, and either a rental casket or a cremation casket.

Traditional Funeral Home - $4000 - $6000

Professional Discount Provider - $2500 - $4000

Internet Provider – NA

Contemporary Cremation

A Contemporary Cremation is basically a funeral service without the body present. The urn and the ashes would be present, but there would've been no viewing or casketed body. You still are selecting Professional Services of Funeral Director and Staff and Use of Facilities, but you'll be saving considerably because there is no Embalming, Other Preparation of Body or cremation casket to purchase.

Traditional Funeral Home - $3000 - $5000

Professional Discount Provider - $1500 - $3000

Internet Provider – NA

Basic Cremation with Private Viewing

Just because you're opting for Basic Cremation doesn't mean you cannot have an opportunity to view the deceased" one more time." Most cremation providers offer a "Private Viewing" package. This would consist of the body being bathed and dressed, presented in an affordable cremation casket, and open to a limited number of immediate family and friends, not to exceed one hour.

Traditional Funeral Home - $2000 - $4000

Professional Discount Provider - $800 - $1600

Internet Provider - $500 - $700

Basic Cremation

This is the least expensive and simplest of the options. This service includes transportation of the deceased at the time of death, filing the death certificate and other associated permits and notifications, cremation container, temporary urn and (perhaps) an online obituary.

Traditional Funeral Home - $2000 - $4000

Professional Discount Provider - $800 - $1600

Internet Provider - $500 - $700

Keep in mind, although many cremation providers include the cost of the cremation container and temporary urn, some may choose to itemize these charges, which would affect the bottom line. Also, many providers do not own a crematory, so the "crematory fee" may be additional. This is usually a minimum of $250. So, when pricing a Basic Cremation, ask if the Merchandise and Crematory Fee is included.

CHAPTER 12

Planning Ahead

You've been given a lot of information in this little book, and there's more in the Appendix. This last chapter will help when planning, preparing for or arranging Deathcare. Remember, it's not only ok to ask questions, it is essential.

Gather Information for the Obituary and Death Certificate:

- Name, address, date and place of birth, and to whom (including mother's maiden name)
- Marital information, including the current marital status; you don't have to mention a divorce in the obituary, but the funeral director needs to know for the death certificate.
- Number of children, grandchildren, great-grandchildren, brothers, sisters, and other relatives
- Relatives who have preceded in death
- Educational background (number of years education for the death certificate)

- Work history, clubs, memberships, organizations (community & professional)
- Hobbies and life-relevant interests
- Social Security number and veteran's history (if applicable, locate the DD 214, which is commonly known as "discharge papers")
- Number of "certified" death certificates you'll need, depending on the financial situation and amount of assets to be disposed, number of life insurance companies, number of cars, truck, boat titles, etc., to be transferred, retirement accounts, and number of different financial institutions

Your Final Wishes and How They Are to be Carried Out:

For burial:

- What type of service: Traditional funeral with viewing (evening before or same day as service), without viewing, private or public service at the funeral home, your church, cemetery chapel or graveside?

- What type of casket: Hardwood or metal? (Review Chapter 5 "Merchandise, Caskets" to make an informed decision)
- What type of vault: Remember to ask your funeral director if one is required by the cemetery. (If it is not a requirement, but you wish to purchase one, please refer to Chapter 6, "Merchandise, Vaults" to make an informed decision)
- For a traditional service, remember to think of the following items: Times and locations of visitation and service; musical selections (usually CDs at the funeral home, organist and vocalist at church); floral tributes (casket spray from the spouse and children and usually a separate, but matching piece from the grandchildren)
- Pallbearers: (Four to six is an ideal number but you may have eight. If you don't want to exclude anyone, consider "honorary pallbearers" who can line up behind the casket when processing)
- Clothing: (Refer to Chapter 7)

- Published obituary: to which papers, whether it is "free" or "paid"; remember to budget a certain amount and have the funeral director edit it as necessary

Selecting the Type of Cremation:

- Immediate or "Direct," which means there is no service or viewing of any kind
- A cremation with a memorial service, which is basically a "direct" cremation, but with a public or private "Memorial Celebration" (the deceased body is not present)
- A traditional viewing and service (embalming is required for public viewing), followed by cremation (remember a cremation casket or a "rental" would have to be selected)
- A private viewing for one hour (embalming is not required), followed by cremation
- Any of the above, followed by a graveside service in which the urn will be interred
- Select an urn which fits your needs: for burial, display on a shelf, stored in a closet or drawer because you're not comfortable looking at it.

When Pre-Paying:

- Ask how it will be funded; through a life insurance company or a trust.
- What is the history with this life insurance company or trust organization? Have they been in business for decades or just a few short years?
- Be aware of which parts of the contract are "guaranteed" and "non-guaranteed."
- Ask if the contract is transferrable if the funeral home sells, goes out of business, or you decide to re-locate.
- Will you receive correspondence from this company, the funeral home, or both, regarding the status of your agreement?
- If you change your plans, what will be the financial consequences? Will there be "administrative fees" in doing so? With an insurance-funded contract, what will the "cash value" be if canceled?

Key Reminders:

- Never feel pressured. If you are not comfortable with a certain funeral director, express it or ask to work with someone else.

- Remember funerals are for the living. You can respect the wishes of the dead and still do what's comfortable for you.
- Think about a budget, tell the funeral director what it is, and have him or her help you stay within it.
- The only "non-declinable" option is "Professional Services of Funeral Director and Staff." Everything else, from "Automobiles" to "Facilities" is "declinable."
- Caskets: You can cut the cost of the casket in half if you request to see more choices. There are identical caskets made of different materials which look the same.
- Vaults: Focus on the 3 least expensive. You will get what you need (or required by the cemetery) with any one of these.
- Out of town death: Call your funeral director back home. DO NOT call a funeral home in the current location. Your funeral director back home will sub-contract the necessary help needed to get the deceased home, and you will save $1500 - $2000.
- Other tasks dealing with the VA and Social Security should be handled by the funeral director. If assistance

Chapter 12: Planning Ahead

is needed in filing insurance claims, that is part of our job also; don't be afraid to ask for help and there should be no additional charges.

APPENDIX

Review: Caskets

It's important to remember when planning a funeral with a burial, the best way to cut back on expenses is by selecting the right merchandise. I will site a few examples:

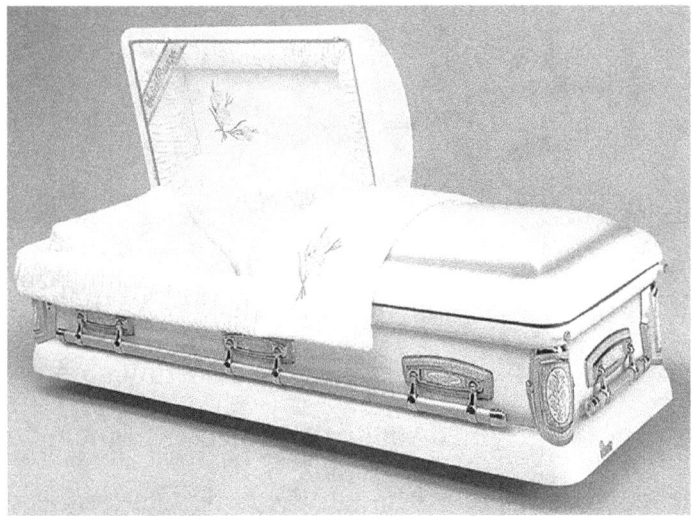

This is the Primrose Bronze casket by Batesville. As the name implies, it is made of solid bronze, has velvet interior with a feminine theme, and is guaranteed never to rust because of the precious metal with which it is built. This casket could easily retail for **$9000-$10,000** at any funeral home. It's a beautiful unit which any funeral home would be glad to sell. The profit margin is quite good. I'm not arguing about a profit margin. Businesses need to make money. But buyer beware, it's not cheap.

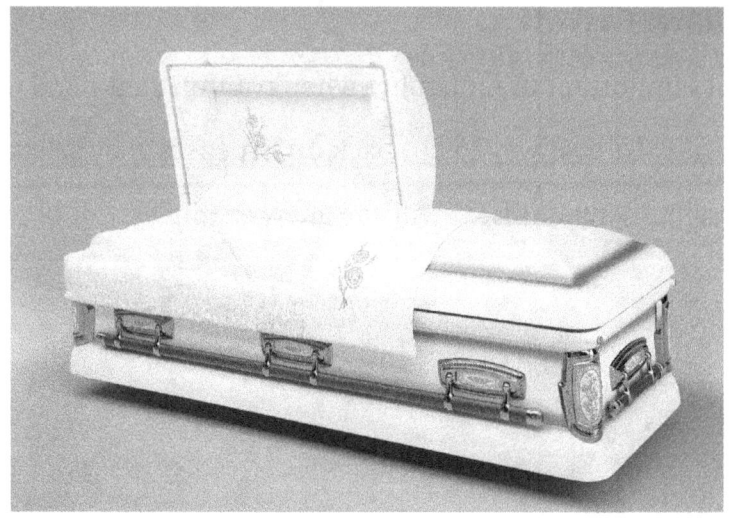

This is the same casket, only manufactured with 18-gauge steel. By its very nature, it could rust over time, but placing it in an affordable, lined vault will protect it from any moisture from the outside. Although the body will lose its water through natural decomposition, this casket comes with a "tray" on the bottom which will protect the integrity of the steel. It is also much more affordable, retailing for **$4000-$5000**; a substantial savings.

APPENDIX

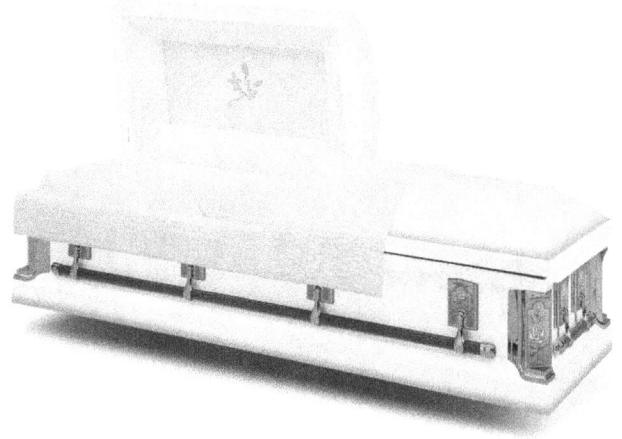

This is the Primrose casket by the same manufacturer, only made of 20-gauge steel, which is a bit thinner. It has the same aesthetic features but instead of a velvet interior, it is a crepe interior, which is much less expensive. This, along with the thinner metal, makes this casket much more affordable, retailing for **$1800-$2800.**

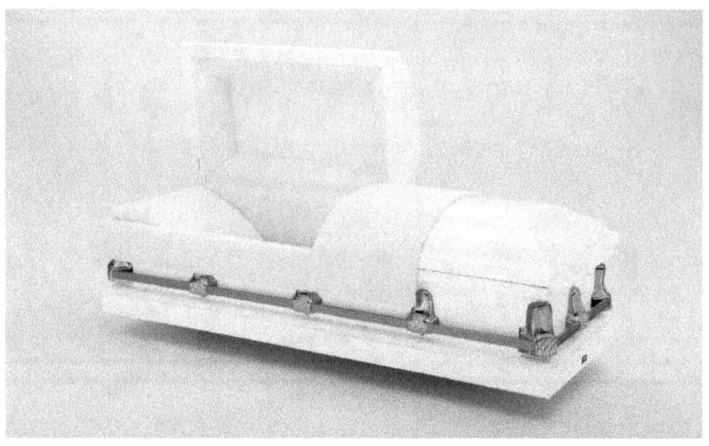

If you want to save even more, consider NewPointe caskets, which are very similar in theme, simple, and still attractive. Depending on the funeral home, this casket could retail for **less than $1000.**

Review: Vaults

When making burial arrangements, the cemetery may require the casket be placed in an "outer burial container" or "vault." ***This is not a state law***, but rather a cemetery requirement in most cases. The above vault is the Wilbert Bronze. It is made of concrete and is triple reinforced—besides the concrete construction, it is lined with a heavy-duty plastic liner, and an additional bronze liner. This is the top-of-the-line vault and will retail **for $15,000-$20,000.**

This is the Venetian by Wilbert. It is a very fine single reinforced burial vault with a heavy-duty liner with the look of polished marble. There are other vaults above this line, but below the Bronze, but in my opinion, there is no need to purchase anything better. This is the vault in which I buried my parents. Their caskets will be adequately protected for eternity. The cost of this vault will be in **the $2,000-$2,500** range.

For the money, this is my favorite vault—the Wilbert Monticello. Although it is considered "basic protection," it is constructed with concrete, has the heavy-duty liner and, like the others, has a "tongue and groove" seal where the lid meets the body. It will be painted to match the casket and provides the protection needed from the weight of the earth above it. All the heavy-duty liners I have described are seamless, which will prevent water from entering the vault, should it penetrate the seams of the concrete. This vault retails for **$1,200-$1,500**—a very good value for those who indeed want the casketed remains to be protected.

APPENDIX

The above container is not considered a vault. It is a concrete grave liner. This grave liner will satisfy the minimum requirements of the cemetery, should there be any. There is nothing fancy about this container. It is literally just a concrete box. It affords no protection from water or other outside elements but will protect the casket from the weight of the earth above it. It can usually be purchased for less than $1,000.

About the Author

Joseph G. Kalmer's formal funeral service education and training can be described as a "baptism by fire." Learning the funeral industry in Chicago is as about as real as it gets, and it started on day one. From living in the basement of a west-side funeral home to working in the Cook County Morgue one day a week, he learned in a hurry that a small-town kid from southern Illinois can make it in this business if he can stomach "the smell of death" literally 24 hours a day.

Joe has been a licensed funeral director and embalmer for 30 years. He is the former owner and operator of Pletcher Funeral Home in Edwardsville, IL, the type of funeral home he refers to as a "traditional" home. Much to the chagrin of his wife, Cheryl, their living quarters were above the funeral home, with the master bedroom directly above the casketed remains in the chapel below.

Joe recognized the changes affecting the funeral industry, such as a rise in cremation and other "less traditional" forms of service. He realized that someday it would be difficult to make a living competing with four other local funeral homes for the 200 annual deaths occurring in his community. So, he opted, himself, for a change.

Welcome to his "Practical Funeral Home." Unlike the days of yesteryear, he is giving the consumers not only the choices they demand, but at a price they can *all* afford. Although he doesn't apologize for the high cost of funerals, he shows you how cremations can cost less than $1000 and casketed funerals can cost less than $5000, never sacrificing the professionalism and dignity everyone deserves.

Joe lives in Edwardsville, Illinois with his wife, Cheryl. They have two daughters, a son-in-law and a granddaughter.